The Cheeky Chins'

Guide To LIFE

ISBN 978-0-244-35197-7

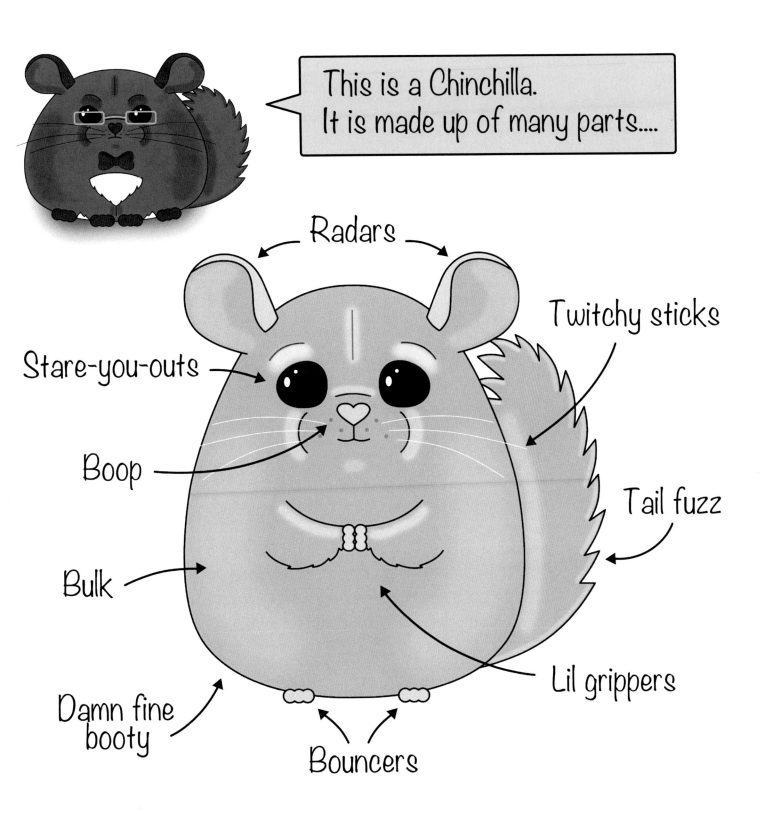

Sleeping. The best way to spend the day! For the best day's sleep you may wish to try these popular positions...

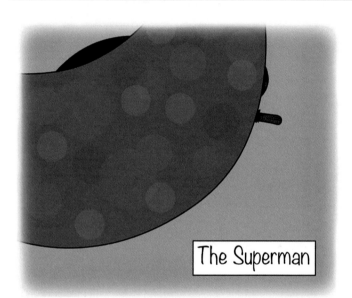

The Superman

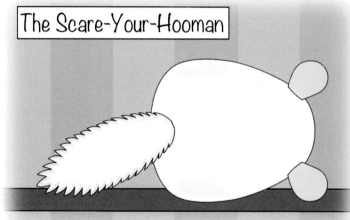

The Scare-Your-Hooman

The Dangle

The Bread Bun

The X-Rated

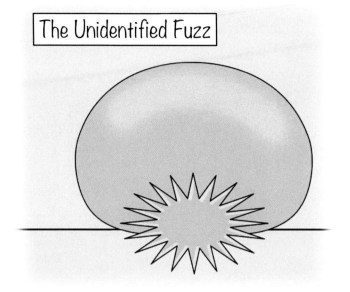

The Unidentified Fuzz

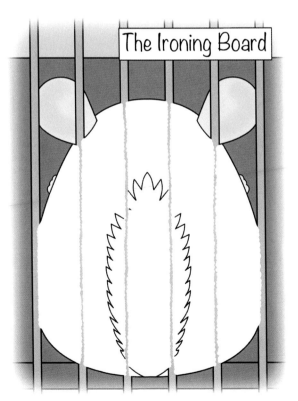

The Ironing Board

The Half-In

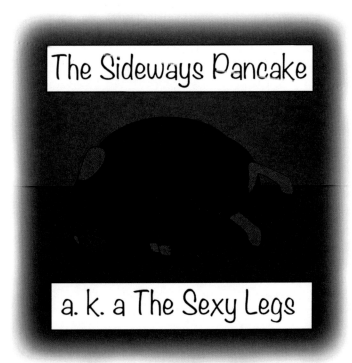

The Sideways Pancake

a. k. a The Sexy Legs

The Totem Pole

The Yin Yang Smoosh

The No Ears

Photographs. The Hoomans are obsessed with taking photographs. They want them to look like this......

..... Unless treats are involved however, the photos the Hoomans take should look like this.....

Keeping clean. Because we are clearly gorgeous we need to keep this fuzz looking good! and here's how to do it...

1. Boxing Lessons

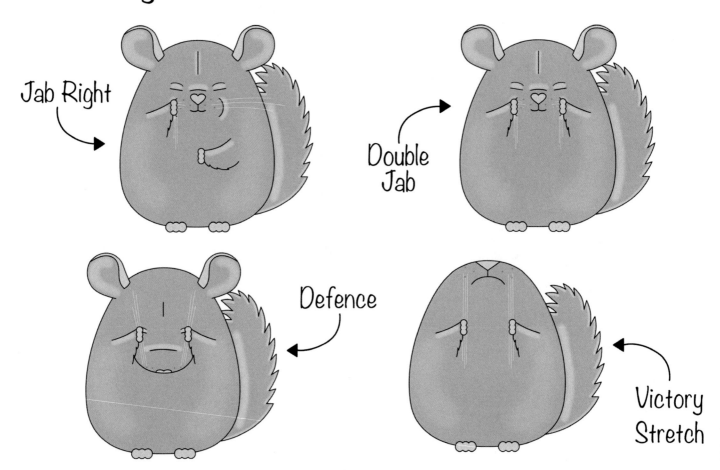

Jab Right

Double Jab

Defence

Victory Stretch

2. Drop and roll!

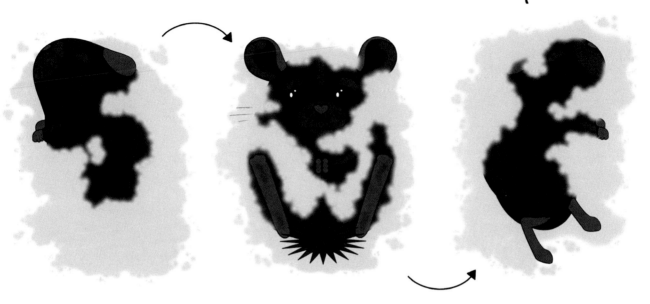

3. Get a friend to chew your head!

We look good. All day every day. We don't even need to try. But to show the Hoomans just how cute we are you can do the following...

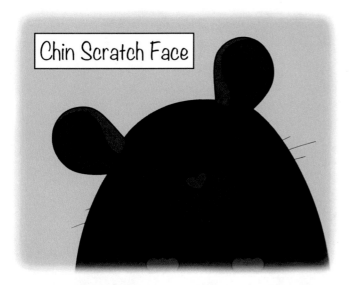

Chin Scratch Face

Squidgy Sleep Pose

Pull the Angel Face

Props, Props, Props...

The Squeaky Sneeze

Wave Your Legs in the Air

Like You Don't Care...

The Glass Sit

The Stretch-and-Yawn

Hats! Lots of hats!

The Cuddle Buddy Smoosh

The Pensive Munch

Signing

The Hoomans - They think they know what they're doing! But sometimes they need our help...

1. Teach them the value of money...

3. Lend a helping hand with their work...

4. Share with them your expertise in home decor...

5. Help with finances...

6. Teach them to appreciate nature...

Help them pick out suitable soft furnishings

How to identify good hay...

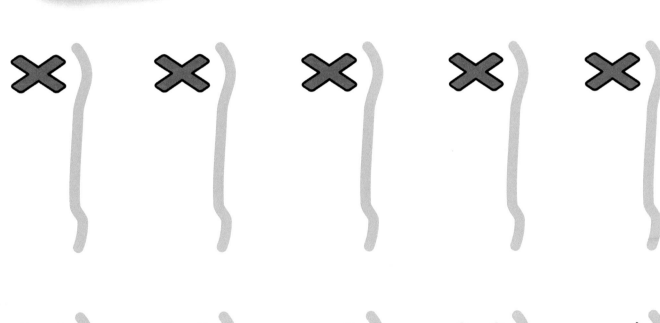

Musical

Interlude

Written in the Stars...

Aries
March 21st - April 19th

Fast and bouncy
Determined
Grumpy
Likes treats

Taurus
April 20th - May 20th

Dislikes cage changes
Hides food
Works hard
Likes treats

Written in the Stars...

Gemini
May 21st - June 20th

Nosy
Quick learner
Enjoys cuddles
Likes treats

Cancer
June 21st - July 22nd

Likes to hide
Love their mum
Suspicious
Likes treats

Written in the Stars...

Roar!

Leo
July 23rd - August 22nd

Lazy
Hates being ignored
Funny
Likes treats

Virgo
August 23rd - September 22nd

Shy
Picky with food
Often on edge
Likes treats

Written in the Stars...

Libra
September 23rd - October 22nd

Likes company
Gentle
Often pouts
Likes treats

Scorpio
October 23rd - November 21st

Jealous
Brave
Good fighters
Likes treats

Written in the Stars...

Sagittarius
November 22nd - December 21st

Impatient
Likes to run wild
Enthusiastic
Likes treats

Capricorn
December 22nd - January 19th

Know-it-all
Born leaders
Hold Grudges
Likes treats

Written in the Stars...

Aquarius
January 20th - February 18th

Independent
Aloof
Eccentric
Likes treats

Pisces
February 19th - March 20th

Intuative
Nervous
Cuddly
Likes treats

Poop. A multifaceted tool. Always keep a good collection of poo to hand, and don't let the Hooman's steal it!

An additional source of nutrition...

Ammunition against the enemy...

Decoration for an otherwise dull room...

Thug Life. Don't let the Hoomans think that they are in charge. Show them who's boss. It's for their own good...

When the Hooman says no...

No!

Stop and turn...

Maintain eye contact...

Chew!

When the Hoomans try to pet you...

Humour them briefly...

Tell them when it's time to leave...

If they don't go, show them the booty!

When the Hoomans "tidy" your home...

Put it back how you like it!

Affection. Throw the Hoomans a bone every now and again and groom them to make them feel good...

Ow......

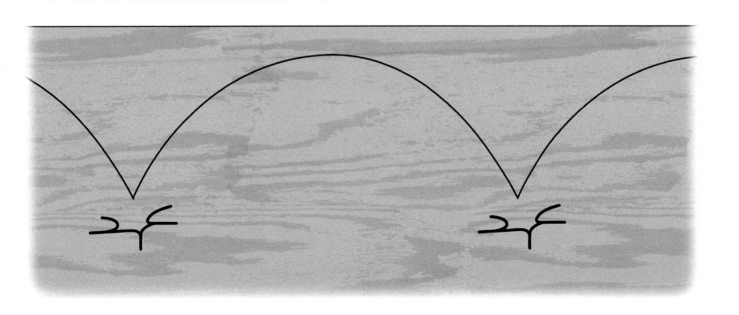

Made in the USA
Las Vegas, NV
30 November 2021